MARTIN LUTHER KING JR. DAY

A TRUE BOOK

by

Dana Meachen Rau

Children's Press®

A Division of Scholastic Inc.

New York Toronto London Auckland Sydney
Mexico City New Delhi Hong Kong
Danbury, Connecticut

Subject Consultant
Melvin Sylvester
Professor
Long Island University

Martin Luther King Jr.

Library of Congress Cataloging-in-Publication Data

Rau, Dana Meachen, 1971-
    Martin Luther King Jr. Day / by Dana Meachen Rau.
        p.   cm. — (a true book)
    Includes bibliographical references and index.
    ISBN 0-516-22246-5 (lib. bdg.)   0-516-27344-2 (pbk.)
I. Martin Luther King Jr. Day—Juvenile literature. 2. King, Martin Luther,
Jr., 1929-1968—Juvenile literature. [I. King, Martin Luther, Jr., 1929-1968.
2. Civil rights workers. 3. Clergy. 4. Afro-Americans—Biography. 5. Martin
Luther King, Jr., Day. 6. Holidays.] I. Title. II. Series.
E185.97.K5 R38 2001
323'.092—dc21
[B]
                                                                    00-060249

© 2001 by Children's Press®
A Division of Scholastic Inc.
Printed in the United States of America.
1 2 3 4 5 6 7 8 9 10 R 10 09 08 07 06 05 04 03 02 01

Contents

A Special Holiday   5

Segregation   8

Martin Luther King Jr.   10

The Montgomery Bus Boycott   14

Using Words, Not Fists   18

Working for Peace   22

Remembering a Great Man   35

To Find Out More   44

Important Words   46

Index   47

Meet the Author   48

Martin Luther King Jr.
(1929–1968)

Coretta Scott King in 1996

Martin went on to Crozer Theological Seminary in Pennsylvania and graduated in 1951. Two years later he married Coretta Scott. In 1954, he became the minister of the Dexter Avenue Baptist Church in Montgomery, Alabama.

13

The Montgomery Bus Boycott

Martin and other black leaders believed that all Americans, including black Americans, should have the same basic rights, or civil rights.

On December 1, 1955, a black woman named Rosa Parks was asked by a bus driver to move to the back of the bus or stand up

Rosa Parks (center) at a march in the 1960s

in order to give her seat to a white passenger. Rosa Parks refused to move and was arrested for not obeying the segregation law.

The people of Montgomery were very upset. They formed the Montgomery Improvement

Association (MIA), and elected Martin as its president. The people wanted to change Montgomery's unfair law about "colored" sections for black bus passengers. Martin and the MIA started a bus boycott. The black people of Montgomery decided not to ride the buses until the law was changed. This became known as the famous Montgomery Bus Boycott. The boycott lasted for 382 days. The black bus passengers took taxis, walked, or carpooled to work and other places.

On February 23, 1956, Martin was arrested for leading the Montgomery Bus Boycott. He was released a few weeks later.

On November 13, 1956, the United States Supreme Court ruled that segregation on Alabama buses was unfair and should be changed. On December 27, 1956, public buses were no longer segregated in Montgomery.

Using Words, Not Fists

Martin believed strongly in nonviolence. He thought words worked better than fists or guns to spread his ideas. Martin learned this from a great leader in India, named Mohandas Gandhi.

By 1957, Martin had become well known for his peaceful

ideas. Ministers throughout the South came to work with him and to learn about how his group succeeded in the boy-cott. On January 12, 1957, Martin helped create the Southern Christian Leadership Conference (SCLC). This group spread news of civil rights around the South. Martin urged people to share the message of equality in nonviolent ways.

From 1957 to 1959, Martin traveled over 780,000 miles

making speeches. In 1958, he wrote his first book, *Stride Toward Freedom.*

Black people were still not allowed to eat in the same restaurants or at the same lunch counters as white people because of their color. Young people also wanted to be a part of this movement led by Martin. So southern black college students formed the Student Nonviolent Coordinating Committee (SNCC) and started a sit-in movement. These students

(From left to right) Joseph McNeill, Franklin McCain, Billy Smith, and Clarence Henderson participate in the first lunch counter sit-ins in Greensboro, North Carolina.

took seats at segregated lunch counters and refused to move. Because they did not obey the laws, the students were taken to jail. But the students believed these "sit-ins" were their way to protest bad laws.

Working for Peace

The civil rights movement was gaining strength, and many white students and white ministers joined in the protest for equal rights for black Americans. In 1961, another movement called the Freedom Rides began. These rides tested laws that could allow blacks

Two protestors hold up signs that speak out against segregation.

and whites to ride in buses that were not segregated when crossing from one state to another.

Martin also helped organize freedom marches across the South. People paraded

A freedom choir holds hands and sings "We Shall Overcome" on the steps of a church in Selma, Alabama.

through towns singing songs about freedom. They carried banners and signs that read, "Give us American rights."

One city was determined to keep freedom marchers out of town—Birmingham, Alabama. Martin went against the order not to march there. Because of this, he and many protest marchers were put in jail. From April 12–20, 1963, Martin sat in jail, and during this time, on April 16, he wrote his famous letter, "Letter from a Birmingham Jail."

On May 3, the police wanted to end this march. They let

Three people hold hands to stand up against the water. The force of this water, used by the police, sent many protestors to the ground.

loose trained attack dogs and squirted fire hoses at the marchers. Television pictures of this terrible act made people from around the world angry at what happened. Because of this, across the United States, 800 marches and sit-ins took place. The largest ever in America was in Washington, D.C., on August 28, 1963. More than 250,000 Americans, including blacks, whites, Native Americans, Mexican Americans, and many more, gathered to hear music and speeches for peace and freedom. Martin was the last one to speak. He gave a speech that spoke of his dreams for equality of all people.

"I Have a Dream . . ."

Martin delivering his famous "I Have a Dream" speech at the Lincoln Memorial

Dr. Martin Luther King, Jr. said these memorable words to the crowd in Washington in 1963:

"I have a dream that one day this nation will rise up and live out the true meaning of its creed: '. . . that all men are created equal.' . . . I have a dream that my four little children will one day live in a nation where they will not be judged by the color of their skin but by the content of their character. . . . When we let

A bird's-eye view of all the marchers from the roof of the Lincoln Memorial. Hundreds of other people stood underneath the trees.

[freedom] ring . . . we will be able to speed up that day when all of God's children . . . will be able to join hands and sing in the words of the old Negro spiritual, 'Free at last! Free at last! Thank God Almighty, we are free at last!"

Marchers holding signs as they walk to the Lincoln Memorial to hear Martin speak

Martin and his friend Reverend Ralph Abernathy sit in a Florida jail on June 11, 1964. They were arrested with 16 others for protesting segregation in a restaurant.

The fight for equality and peace was not over. On July 2, 1964, the Congress of the United States passed the Civil Rights Act. It stated that there could no longer be laws against black Americans.

Around the world people saw the good work Martin was doing in America. On December 10, 1964, Martin was presented the Nobel Peace Prize in Oslo, Norway, for his work for peace in the world. Martin was the

Martin holds a case containing the Nobel Peace Prize gold medal after the presentation in Oslo, Norway. Gunnar Jahn, the chairman of the prize, made the presentation.

Martin and his wife Coretta leading a march in 1965

youngest person to ever receive the award.

In 1967, Martin started another movement for poor people. He called it the Poor People's Campaign. On April 3, Martin gave a speech in Memphis, Tennessee, that became known as "I've Been to the Mountaintop."

On April 4, 1968 at six in the evening, just before dinner, Martin stepped out on the balcony of the Lorraine Hotel

The balcony of the Lorraine Motel after Martin was shot in 1968

where he was staying in Memphis. Martin was shot and killed. Later, a man named James Earl Ray was captured and sent to jail for 99 years. Ray died on April 23, 1999.

Remembering a Great Man

Many Americans and supporters from around the world wanted to honor Martin in a special way. On April 8, 1968, Massachusetts Senator Edward W. Brooke introduced a bill in Congress to make January 15, Martin's birthday, a national holiday. Year after year, the bill came before Congress, and year after year it did not have enough votes to become a law.

Coretta Scott King and other black leaders urged Congress to vote for the holiday. They asked people to write letters to Congress showing their support. They presented Congress with petitions signed by more than six million people. They even organized another march to Washington on January 15, 1981.

Even though it wasn't yet a national holiday, many states celebrated Martin Luther King Jr.

Day on January 15. People also honored Martin by naming many buildings, schools, hospitals, streets, and other gathering places after him.

In the presence of Coretta Scott King, President Ronald Reagan signs the bill making Martin Luther King Jr.'s birthday a national holiday. Martin's children stand behind them.

On November 2, 1983, there were finally enough votes in Congress for the holiday. President Ronald Reagan signed the bill that made Martin Luther

King Jr. Day a national holiday.
People now celebrate this day
on the third Monday in January
every year. This day is not only
celebrated in the United States.
Many other countries around the
world also honor Martin.

On Martin Luther King Jr. Day,
schools and many businesses
are closed. Some cities hold
parades. Some groups lead
peaceful marches. Children wave
flags. Men and women give
speeches about Martin. Some

churches hold special services. People might hear Martin's famous "I Have a Dream" speech being played over the radio or on television.

In schools, children often use the week before the holiday to learn about Martin. They talk about his ideas—that all people are created equal; that one's character, and not the color of one's skin, is important; and that problems can be solved without violence.

Parade marchers celebrating Martin's birthday in Seattle, Washington (top); Children marching on the 30th anniversary of Martin's death in Memphis, Tennessee (bottom).

Timeline

1929 Born in Atlanta, Georgia

1948 Graduates from Morehouse College, Georgia

1951 Graduates from Crozer Theological Seminary, Pennsylvania

1953 Marries Coretta Scott

1954 Becomes minister at Dexter Avenue Baptist Church, Montgomery, Alabama

1955 Receives his doctorate degree from Boston University

1955 Elected president of the Montgomery Improvement Association (MIA)

1957 Helps create and is elected president of the Southern Christian Leadership Conference (SCLC)

Coretta Scott King with her children, (from left to right) Martin Luther King III, Yolanda Denise, and Dexter Scott in 1962

1958   Publishes first book, *Stride Toward Freedom*

1963   Writes "Letter from a Birmingham Jail"

1963   Presents "I Have a Dream" speech at march on Washington

1964   Receives the Nobel Peace Prize

1968   Dies in Memphis, Tennessee

1983   Martin Luther King Jr. Day becomes a national holiday

Martin and his wife Coretta leading the Freedom March in 1965. Rosa Parks (far left) marches also.

The Martin Luther King Jr. National Historic Site in Atlanta, Georgia

The grave of Martin Luther King Jr. at the historic site

To Find Out More

Here are some additional resources to help you learn more about Martin Luther King Jr. Day and other holidays:

 **Books**

Celsi, Teresa. **Rosa Parks and the Montgomery Bus Boycott.** The Millbrook Press, 1991.

Hakim, Rita. **Martin Luther King, Jr., and the March Toward Freedom.** The Millbrook Press, 1991.

Lowery, Linda. **Martin Luther King Day.** Carolrhoda Books, 1987.

MacMillan, Dianne M. **Martin Luther King, Jr. Day.** Enslow Publishers, Inc., 1992.

Stein, R. Conrad. **The Assassination of Martin Luther King, Jr.** Children's Press, 1996.

Stein, R. Conrad. **The Montgomery Bus Boycott.** Children's Press, 1993.

Organizations and Online Sites

Festivals.com
RSL Interactive
1101 Alaskan Way
Pier 55, Suite 300
Seattle, WA 98101
http://www.festivals.com

Visit this site to find out about all types of festivals, holidays, and fairs around the world.

The Holiday Zone
http://www.geocities.com/ holidayzone

Find ideas to celebrate your favorite holiday at this site, including Martin Luther King Jr. Day.

Martin Luther King, Jr., National Historic Site
http://www.nps.gov/malu/

At this site, created by the National Parks Service, visit the Martin Luther King Jr. National Historic Site without having to go to Atlanta, or find out information about how to go there on your own.

The Martin Luther King Jr. Papers Project
www.stanford.edu/group/ king

This site holds a collection of King's speeches and letters and information about his life.

Important Words

bill a proposed law

boycott to refuse to do something

civil rights the basic rights all people have to freedom and equality under the law

equality treating everyone the same way

freedom the right to do and say what you like

movement people who have joined together to support a cause

national having to do with a whole country

petition a written request to ask for something

rights something that the law says you can have or do, as in the right to vote

segregation to keep black and white people separate from each other

violence to use physical force to hurt someone

Index

(**Boldface** page numbers indicate illustrations.)

bill, 34, 38
boycott, 14–17, 19
civil rights, 6, 14, 19, 22, 30
Columbus, Christopher, 6, **7**
equality, 7, 8, 19, 22, 28, 30, 40
freedom, 22–25, 27
holiday, 5–6, 35–36, 38–40
King, Coretta Scott, 13, **13, 32**, 36, 42–43, **42, 43**
King, Martin Luther, Jr.
  assassination of, 34
  early life, 10–12

honoring, 5–6, 31, 35–41
jailing, 17, 25, 30
photos of, **4, 17, 28, 30, 31, 32**
speeches, 20, 27–29, 33, 40
marches, 23–29, 36, 39, **41**
movement, 20, 22, 33
national, 35, 36, 39
Nobel Peace Prize, 31, 33
Parks, Rosa, 14–15, **15**
petition, 36
rights, 8, 14, 24, 46. *See also* civil rights
segregation, 8–9, 14–15, 17, 20–21, 23
sit-ins, 20–21, **21,** 27
Washington, George, 6, **7**

Meet the Author

Ever since Dana Meachen Rau can remember, she has loved to write. A graduate of Trinity College in Hartford, Connecticut, Dana works as a children's book editor and has authored more than thirty books for children, including biographies, nonfiction, early readers, and historical fiction. She has also won writing awards for her short stories.

When Dana is not writing, she is spending time with her husband, Chris, and son, Charlie, in Farmington, Connecticut.